MUSIQUE CONCRÈTE

by

David Ernst

Crescendo Publishing Company

Boston, Massachusetts

MUSIQUE CONCRÈTE

by

David Ernst

Crescendo Publishing Company
Boston, Massachusetts

ISBN 87597-081-8
Library of Congress Card Number 72-87761
Printed in the United States of America
© 1972 Crescendo Publishing Company

CONTENTS

Preface   i

Chapter I: Introduction   1

Chapter II: Basic Concepts   3

Chapter III: Developments Leading to First
              Electronic Music Compositions   6

Chapter IV: Survey of Musique Concrète 10

Chapter V: Exercises in Composition   20

Chapter VI: Discography   29

Bibliography   32

Index   34

PREFACE

The purpose of this book is to provide both teachers and students with enough information to begin study in the field of musique concrète.

The first five chapters are arranged so that they may be divided into five units of work, and the final chapter contains an extensive discography that may be used in conjunction with chapter IV. A bibliography is also included, and it contains both books and articles that are suitable for teachers and students.

Chapter I is concerned with the elementary physics of sound, and it is sufficient for a basic understanding of the scientific principles behind electronic music. More detailed information may be obtained from the books and articles contained in the bibliography.

Chapter II proceeds to discuss the actual procedures involved in the production of musique concrète compositions, while the next chapter traces the scientific, musical, and historical developments that led to the establishment of the first electronic music studio in 1948.

Chapter IV discusses some 21 musique concrète compositions in detail, and record numbers and prices are also included.

Chapter V contains five graded exercises in tape composition to help students actually compose their own musique concrète pieces, with continual references to previous chapters and discussions. The only materials needed are two tape recorders, microphone, and associated inexpensive materials, all of which are generally available at most schools.

It is hoped that this book will be of value to all those who are interested in electronic music, for it begins with basic concepts and develops into a thorough discussion

of the composers, music, and techniques involved with this
field. This book also provides the reader with sufficient
knowledge to create his own compositions with a minimal
amount of equipment.

                                                    D.E.

Chapter I

INTRODUCTION

Everything that we hear is sound, and these sounds travel through the air in the form of WAVES, e.g. ⌢⌣⌢⌣ , ⌢⌣⌢⌣ . The waves may be of any shape, but the larger the wave is, the louder it will be. For example, wave 'a' is louder that 'b,' therefore 'a' is said to be of greater AMPLITUDE than wave 'b.'

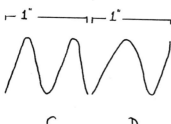

A   B

Another property of sound waves is the number of times they occur within a certain amount of time. Since 'c' occurred twice within one second and 'd' occurred only once within the same amount of time, 'c' is of a higher pitch than 'd.' Another name for pitch is FREQUENCY, so the frequency of 'c' is higher than that of 'd.'

C   D

The frequency, however, can be measured in terms of CPS (cycles per second) or Hz (Hertz). No matter which system is employed, the time interval of one second is always used as the standard. The frequency of 'c,' then, would be 2 Hz, and that of 'd' is 1 Hz.

Unfortunately, our ears are not sensitive enough to hear such low sounds, for the range of human hearing is between 16 Hz and 20,000 Hz. Dogs and some other animals, on the other hand, are much more sensitive to frequencies above 20,000 Hz.

Sine

Square

Sawtooth

Chapter II

BASIC CONCEPTS

There are three main types of electronic music: musique concrète; music by synthesisers(1); and computer music(2). This book deals solely with MUSIQUE CONCRETE, which involves the use of tape recorders and tape manipulations to record and modify any type of sound.

The technical knowledge needed to operate a tape recorder in order to produce tape compositions will be covered in Chapter V, but the following information will serve as an introduction to some basic concepts and terminology used in the area of electronic music.

All electronic equipment, including tape recorders, is based upon the principle of input and output. Any sounds being fed into the tape recorder are called INPUT SIGNALS, and they may be obtained either by use of a microphone, another tape recorder, or other electronic equipment.

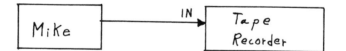

(1). Some currently available synthesisers are the ARP, Moog, Putney, and the Electric Music Box.
(2). Computer programs are available from Bell Telephone Laboratories and from Stanford University.

All sounds that are emitted from the tape recorder
are OUTPUT SIGNALS, and they eventually reach our ears
through the use of loudspeakers. Two typical situations
involving tape recorders are as follows:

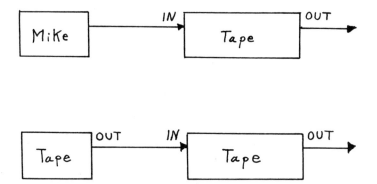

When connecting a microphone to a tape recorder, the
microphone must be plugged into the Input jack of the
recorder (see diagrams above). Notice that inputs are
connected only to outputs, and not to other inputs. The
same procedure applies when connecting one tape recorder to
another.

The opportunity to make either MONAURAL (1 channel)
or STEREO (2 channels) recordings is also available on most
tape recorders. The diagrams above represent a monaural
set-up, for they involve only one input and one output.
Since stereo involves two channels, there must be two inputs
and two outputs.

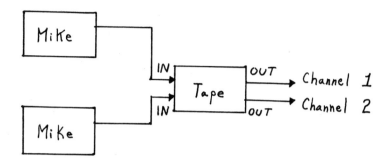

        Most tape recorders also have a VU METER, which indi-
cates the amplitude of the input signal. If the indicator
moves into the upper third of the meter there will probably
be some distortion on the tape, so the volume control on the
tape recorder should be turned down when this occurs. On
the other hand, if the indicator fails to move at all, the
input signal probably is not loud enough. When this occurs
turn up the volume on the tape recorder.

Chapter III

DEVELOPMENTS LEADING TO FIRST ELECTRONIC
MUSIC COMPOSITIONS

The first electronic music studio was established in 1948 in Paris by Pierre Schaeffer, but it was preceded by a long line of discoveries and inventions dating back to the 14th century. One of the first of these was the CARILLON, which was first found in Belgium and the Netherlands. The carillon consisted of a series of pegs placed on a rotating drum, and as the drum turned the pegs struck some tuned bells. Since the bells were stationary, the position of the pegs determined which bells were to be struck.

In 1644 the HYDRAULIC ORGAN was invented by the French engineer de Caus, and it was basically a development of the principles of the carillon. The hydraulic organ also had a revolving drum with pegs, but a water wheel provided the energy to turn the drum, and the pegs activated a series of keys, not bells. The keys then allowed air to flow into a set of organ pipes which then produced the sound.

During the next century Benjamin Franklin developed the GLASS HARMONICA (1763), and both Mozart and Beethoven used this instrument in some of their compositions. The glass harmonica had a series of revolving glass discs which were kept wet by passing through a trough of water. The performer made the discs revolve by using a foot pedal, and sound was produced by lightly touching the edge of the glass with the fingers. The glass discs became progressively thicker so that a high pitch was obtained from the thin ones, and a lower pitch resulted from the thicker discs.

From the late 19th century onward mechanical and electronic inventions flourished. Alexander Bell invented the telephone in 1876, and two years later Thomas Edison invented the PHONOGRAPH (1878). The principle upon which the phonograph was based was that since all sounds travel in the form of waves (Ch. I), it should then be possible to

somehow record these waves. Edison accomplished this by
transferring speech vibrations (waves) to a diaphragm,
needle, and a strip of paraffin-coated paper. The needle
then cut grooves in the paraffin, and the sounds were
permanently recorded.

        In 1897 Vortez developed the PIANOLA, which used a
pre-punched roll of paper to activate a set of keys by use
of air bellows. There were eighty-eight such keys (like a
piano), and they were placed directly over a piano keyboard.
The keys of the pianola struck the keys of the piano by the
use of air pressure which was controlled by the paper roll.

        The beginning of the 20th century was marked by the
"art of noises" concerts (1914) in Milan by Luigi Russolo.
Russolo designed and built his own instruments which were
called INTONARUMORI--noise instruments. Most of these were
built in very large cases, and they made a variety of noise-
like sounds such as grunts and hisses. The Intonarumori
were used by Russolo to accompany traditional music, so that
the result was a bizarre combination of traditional music
and noise sounds.

        Following this, in the 1920's, more composers began
introducing new types of sounds in their compositions. The
French composer Darius Milhaud experimented with changing
the speeds of phonograph records in order to obtain trans-
formations of recorded sounds (1922-1927). In 1924 the
Italian composer Respighi wrote the PINES OF ROME, in which
he called for a phonograph recording of nightingales to play
in conjunction with a symphony orchestra. Finally, in 1927,
another French composer, Antheil, wrote the BALLET
MECHANIQUE. In this piece Antheil utilized car horns,
airplane propellers, saws, and anvils.

        One of the most valuable inventions to the field of
electronic music was the TAPE RECORDER (1935) by Allgemeine
Elektrizitäts Gesellschaft. Without this instrument electronic music would have virtually been non-existent.

        Until this time most of the composers involved with
mechanical/electronic procedures in their compositions were
European. One of the first American composers to have much
influence in this area was John Cage, who in 1939 wrote his
IMAGINARY LANDSCAPE NO. 1. The sound sources for this composition were a muted piano, cymbal, and two variable-speed
phonographs playing Victor test recordings. One of the most
important aspects of this work was the changing concept of a
traditional concert, for Cage intended the IMAGINARY LAND-
SCAPE to be performed either as a recording or a radio
broadcast.

Finally, in 1948, the French radio broadcaster Pierre Schaeffer established the first electronic music studio. It was located in Paris, and it quickly drew the attention of many important composers, including Pierre Henry, Luciano Berio, and Karlheinz Stockhausen.

The following table chronologically outlines both the musical events discussed in this chapter and some corresponding historical events.

	MUSIC	HISTORY
14th Cent.	Carillons in Belgium and Netherlands.	Dante - DIVINE COMEDY (1307); Hundred Years' War (1337); Black Plague (1348); Chaucer - CANTERBURY TALES (1386).
1644	de Caus - Hydraulic Organ.	End of Thirty Years' War (1648).
1763	Franklin - Glass Harmonica.	Canada ceded to England.
1878	Edison - Phonograph.	Bell - Telephone (1876).
1897	Vortez - Pianola.	Spanish-American War (1898).
1914	Russolo - ART OF NOISES.	World War I; Panama Canal opened.
1922	Milhaud - phonograph speed changes.	Fascist revolution in Italy; Discovery of insulin.
1924	Respighi - PINES OF ROME.	Stalin becomes dictator in Russia.
1927	Antheil - BALLET MECHANIQUE.	Lindbergh's solo flight across Atlantic; first television transmission.
1935	AEG - First tape recorder.	Hitler becomes Fuhrer in Germany (1934).
1939	Cage - IMAGINARY LANDSCAPE.	World War II.
1948	Schaeffer - First electronic music studio.	First assembly of United Nations (1946); Korean War (1950).

Chapter IV

SURVEY OF MUSIQUE CONCRETE

Most of the compositions discussed in this chapter
are available on commercial recordings. The record numbers
and prices are included when this is the case.

The first electronic music studio to be established
was founded by Pierre Schaeffer in Paris in 1948.
Schaeffer, working for the Radiodiffusion-Television
Francaise (R.T.F.) as a broadcaster, began his studio with
the facilities at the R.T.F.--variable-speed tape recorders
and phonographs, microphones, and sound-effects records.
The first electronic music, therefore, was composed solely
with this equipment, and it has since been termed musique
concrète--transformation of natural sounds by tape
manipulations.

Schaeffer's first compositions were completed in
1948, and the earliest ones were very short in length. Five
works from this period are: ETUDE AUX CHEMINS DE FER (CON-
CERT OF LOCOMOTIVES), which was based on sound-effects
recordings of locomotives; ETUDE AUX TOURNIQUETS, in which
Schaeffer used a xylophone, bells, toy whistling tops, and
variable-speed phonographs as his sound sources; ETUDE AU
PIANO I and ETUDE AU PIANO II, which were based on a series
of chords played on a piano and then transformed by means of
tape manipulations; ETUDE AUX CASSEROLES, which used
spinning covers from pans, canal boats, spoken and sung
sounds, harmonicas, and a piano.

The choice of sounds that Schaeffer employed in these
early works shows not only a great imagination, but an
increased awareness for all types of sounds. Composers were
now beginning to think in terms of 'pure' sound, and they
were no longer restricted to using only the standard orches-
tral instruments.

In 1949 Schaeffer was joined by another French composer, Pierre Henry, and the following year they collaborated to compose the SYMPHONIE POUR UN HOMME SEUL (SYMPHONY FOR A MAN ALONE).

Pierre Schaeffer and Pierre Henry: SYMPHONIE POUR UN HOMME SEUL (1950); DUC-9 @ $5.98.
SYMPHONIE exists in two versions. It was originally conceived as a solo tape composition but was then revised, divided into eleven sequences, and choreographed for a ballet by the famous Frenchman, Maurice Béjart. Béjart was later to work with Pierre Henry choreographing many of Henry's tape compositions--ASTROLOGIE, VARIATIONS FOR A DOOR AND A SIGH, LE VOYAGE, and MASS FOR TODAY.

The eleven sections of SYMPHONIE are as follows: Prosopopee I, Partita, Valse, Erotica, Scherzo, Prosopopee II, Eroica, Apostrophe, Intermezzo, Cadence, and Strette.

It is interesting to observe how these early musique concrete pieces tended to rely either on some pre-established musical forms such as the valse, partita, scherzo etc., or else on an extra-musical form as the ballet. Since the earlier electronic compositions were relatively short the problem of having a large over-all form was not present. Once the pieces became longer however, more consideration had to be given to formal divisions, for these composers were no longer dealing with the conventional concepts of pitch and rhythm. They needed some conventions of the past to provide coherence for their work in this new and un-explored territory. More examples of this type of construction are found in the subsequent works of Henry.

Pierre Henry: ASTROLOGIE (ASTROLOGY) (1952); DUC-9 @ $5.98.
This is the first example of musique concrete for a commercial French film, and the music is divided into four sequences--les Etoiles (the stars), les Cataclysmes (the disasters), les Machines (the machines), and la Guerre (the war). The music was composed to accompany a film--another instance of an extra-musical form. This work was also choreographed by Bejart for the ballet ARCANE.

Pierre Henry: ANTIPHONIE (ANTIPHONY) (1952); DUC-9 @ $5.98.
As is the case with most of Henry's works, the title is the key to the whole idea behind the composition. The word 'antiphony,' in the musical sense, means the alternation between two choirs, and in this composition there are two opposing forces grouped as blocks of sound. One group is strictly determined while the other sound block is allowed to evolve freely. At the end of the piece both

blocks are altered and superimposed upon each other.

Pierre Henry: ENTITE (ENTITY) (1959); Limelight LS 86048
       @ $5.98.
       The title again reveals the meaning behind the music,
for in this piece Henry wished to establish a connection
between the paintings of Degottex and sounds. The connection between these two areas--visual and aural--was based on
speed, for we experience speed both with our eyes and our
ears. Notice how the music is still closely related to an
extra-musical form.

Pierre Henry: LE VOYAGE (THE VOYAGE) (1962); Limelight
       LS 86049 @ $5.98.
       This was another ballet for Béjart, and it was based
on the Tibetan BOOK OF THE DEAD. The reading of this book
at one's death assists the dying in their voyage from death
to rebirth. In the Tibetan religion there are three stages
between death and rebirth, and these divisions are also
present in the music--After Death 1 and 2, Peaceful and
Wrathful Deities, and the Coupling. Henry added a section
at the beginning and end, so that the final form of the
music is as follows:

```
            Breath 1
            After Death 1 ─────────────▶ 1st stage
            After Death 2 ─┘
            Peaceful Deities ───────────▶ 2nd stage
            Wrathful Deities ─┘
            The Coupling ───────────────── 3rd stage
            Breath 2
```

       Again, as in most of Henry's pieces, a clearly out-
lined form is present, and this form is based on a religious
book rather than on some purely musical idea.

Pierre Henry: VARIATIONS FOR A DOOR AND A SIGH (1963);
       Limelight LS 86059 @ $5.98.
       This composition has also been choreographed by
Béjart, and the dancers are called upon to improvise. There
are only three sound sources employed in the VARIATIONS--a
sigh (breathing in and out), the striking of a musical saw,
and a creaking door. It was conceived as an improvisatory
ballet for seven dancers, and it consists of 25 short sections in the style of the 17th century French suite. The
movements are as follows: slumber, hesitation, song 1,
awakening, song 2, stretching, gestures, reckoning, fever 1,
yawning, song 3, wrath, hesitation 2, breathing, fever 2,
gymnastics, song 4, wailing, waves, song 5, trance, death-
rattle, snoring, song 6, and death.

-12-

Frenchmen were not the only composers to use the
facilities at the R.T.F., for during the early 1950's there
were very few places for composers to work in the field of
electronic music. The first German studio was opened in
Köln in 1951, and it was not until 1955 that the first
Italian studio was established in Milan. One of the Italian
composers to work in Paris was Luc Ferrari.

Luc Ferrari: VISAGE V (1959); Limelight LS 86047 @ $5.98.
        This piece is another example of a non-musical idea
supplying the over-all form of the music, for it is based on
the actions of a 'Character' and six 'Creatures.' The
'Character' is depicted by a thick, prolonged sound, and the
six 'Creatures' by shorter rhythmic motives. The music is
divided into three sections in the following manner:
    I - "The character and his creatures"--all of the musical
        ideas (sounds) are presented.
   II - "The creatures conceal the character in the earth"--
        the character interferes with the creatures while they
        are playing, so the creatures fight and defeat the
        character. This is expressed musically by super-
        imposing the creature sounds over one another.
  III - "The character in a state of natural purity"--the
        character is transformed.

        Even though it appears to be a simple fairytale on
the surface, there seems to be some hint of a deeper
philosophical meaning, especially in the final section when
the character is transformed into a state of 'natural
purity.' This is very similar to Henry's VOYAGE from death
to rebirth.

        One of the most important composers today is Iannis
Xenakis, who is also an architect. Xenakis was born in
Greece, then lived in France and became a French citizen,
and now teaches at Indiana University.

Iannis Xenakis: CONCRETE P-H II (1958, rev. 1968);
        Nonesuch H 71246 @ $2.98.
        Xenakis created this work for the Philips Pavilion at
the 1958 Brussels World Fair. This record, however, contains the revised version completed in 1968. The sound
source is the noise of smoldering charcoal, which was
recorded and spliced in order to obtain various textures.
The tape was to be played over 400 loudspeakers which were
an integral part of the architectural structure of the
Philips Pavilion. Xenakis worked with the famous French
architect Le Corbusier for about ten years, and both men
were involved with the design of the Philips Pavilion. The
position of the loudspeakers was determined by the pavilion's structure, and the music came from various speakers at

different times, giving the impression of moving sounds. This topic will be covered in greater detail when the music of Varèse is discussed.

Iannis Xenakis: ORIENT-OCCIDENT I (1960); Limelight
        LS 86047 @ $5.98.
        This composition was originally written for a film by UNESCO, and it was revised by Xenakis in 1968. In this piece the composer wanted to depict the feelings of a spectator who had gone back in time, seeing the world of the past. Like the pieces of Henry and Ferrari, the music has a very deep significance, for it does not end with a simple story or idea.

Iannis Xenakis: DIAMORPHOSES II (1957); Nonesuch H 71246
        @ $2.98.
        DIAMORPHOSES is divided into four sections--the first and last being of a very thick texture, while the two inner sections have a much thinner texture. Some of the sounds used are jet planes, railroad cars crashing, earthquake shocks, and both very high and low frequencies.

Iannis Xenakis: BOHOR I (1962); Nonesuch H 71246 @ $2.98.
        The sound sources of this work are very limited, for they consist solely of a Laotian mouth organ and some Oriental bracelets and other jewelry. One of the most interesting aspects of the piece is the gradual crescendo that continues throughout its entirety, for it is not no-ticeable until the piece is almost over. Procedures such as these are definitely based upon the listener's capabilities of sense perception, and there are numerous possibilities in electronics for working in this area. Both BOHOR I and CONCRETE P-H are excellent examples of this.

Iannis Xenakis: ORIENT-OCCIDENT III (1968); Nonesuch
        H 71246 @ $2.98.
        This revised version of ORIENT-OCCIDENT employs a very wide range of sounds, and the results are extremely interesting. The first group of sounds were obtained by drawing a cello bow across various substances such as card-board boxes, metal rods, and gongs. Other sounds were obtained from the ionosphere in the form of electrical sig-nals. Finally, Xenakis played an excerpt from one of his orchestral compositions, PITHOPRAKTA, but this excerpt was played at a slower speed. The resulting sound was still similar to the orchestral music, but at the same time it sounded different. This is one of the characteristics of altering the speed of records and tapes.

        Luciano Berio is one of the most influential com-posers today, and he writes both electronic and

non-electronic music. He founded the Electronic Music
Studio in Milan in 1955, and is currently on the faculty at
the Juilliard School in New York.

Luciano Berio: OMAGGIO A JOYCE (HOMAGE TO JOYCE) (1959);
        Turnabout TV 34177 @ $2.98.
        All of the sounds in this piece are produced by a
female voice speaking the beginning of the eleventh chapter
of James Joyce's ULYSSES in English, Italian, and French. A
great amount of work was involved in tape splicing and other
manipulations, much of which will be discussed in Chapter V.

Luciano Berio: VISAGE (1961); Turnabout TV 34046 @ $2.98,
        and Columbia OS-3320 @ $5.98.
        A female voice again supplies the main material--
laughter, crying, singing, patterns of speech inflections,
and the single Italian word 'parole' (words). This composition is only to resemble intelligible and coherent speech
and, like OMAGGIO A JOYCE, it required a great deal of tape
splicing and manipulations.

        A very important German composer of today is
Karlheinz Stockhausen. He was one of the first to use the
Electronic Music Studio in Köln when it opened in 1951, and
since that time has spent most of his energy working in the
area of electronic music.

Karlheinz Stockhausen: MIKROPHONIE I (1964); Columbia
        MS 7355 @ $5.98.
        In the strict sense of the word, MIKROPHONIE I is not
an example of musique concrete because it does not involve
tape recordings and manipulations. However, because of the
great importance of microphones and external sounds, this
work is included in this book.

        The equipment needed for MIKROPHONIE is a tam
tam(1), two microphones, and two filters(2) and poten-
tiometers(3), and each performance of this piece must be
done 'live'--there are no pre-recorded tapes involved, as
was the case with all of the electronic music discussed so
far. Two performers strike the tam tam with various objects
(wood sticks, metal rods, brushes etc.) while two others
pick up the sound with microphones. There are two main

(1). A tam tam is a large Chinese gong.
(2). A filter is a piece of electronic equipment which is
      capable of cutting out or boosting certain
      frequencies.
(3). A potentiometer is a variable resistor which is like a
      volume control on a radio.

factors which determine the type of sounds picked up by the
microphones:

1. the distance between the microphone and the tam tam.
   If the mike is far away from the tam tam the sound
   that it picks up will be relatively soft, but as the
   microphone is moved closer the amplitude of the signal will increase. Therefore, a crescendo or
   dimuendo can be obtained simply by moving the
   microphone either closer to or farther from the
   tam tam.

2. the rhythm of the movement of the microphone. If
   the microphone remains stationary the result will be
   a 'normal' reproduction of the original sound. On
   the other hand, if the microphone is constantly
   moved (back and forth, circular motion etc.) it may
   pick up disturbances in the air that were created by
   its own movement. Furthermore, moving the microphone gives different perspectives to the sound in
   the same way that different positions give various
   perspectives when looking at a work of sculpture.

The filters further shape the sounds because they are
able to select certain frequencies to be either emphasized
or eliminated. The filters are connected to an amplifier
and loudspeakers, and the speakers are then placed wherever
the composer wishes. Below is a block diagram of the
connections used in this piece.

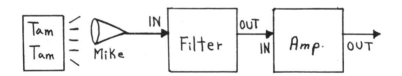

Edgar Varèse was born in France and later moved to
America. Many of his pieces involve a lot of percussion
instruments, and he also spent much time working with electronics. In 1954 he completed DESERTS, which was for tape
and large orchestra. The tape was partly prepared at the
R.T.F. studio in Paris, and partly at the Columbia-Princeton
Tape Center in New York. Varese died in 1965.

Edgar Varèse: POEM ELECTRONIQUE (1958); Columbia MS 6146
        @ $5.98.
        This composition, like Xenakis' CONCRETE P-H, was
composed for the Philips Pavilion at the 1958 Brussels World
Fair. The tape was made up of a variety of electronic
sounds, church bells, organ chords, sirens etc., and it
required 350 loudspeakers for its performance. The loudspeakers were divided into various groups, and the sounds
from the tape were electronically directed to these different groups of speakers. These were called "sound routes."
In addition to this complex set-up there was also an elabo-
rate lighting display including four large film projectors,
eight projection lanterns, six spot lights, six ultra-violet
lamps, fifty electric bulbs representing stars, and several
hundred tubular fluorescent lamps in various colors.
Listening to a recording of the POEME by no means approaches
the original conception of the piece, and it is with this in
mind that one should now listen.

        About the same time that the Köln studio opened in
Germany two American composers began experimenting in New
York with tape compositions. These men were Otto Luening
and Vladimir Ussachevsky, and together they established the
Columbia-Princeton Electronic Music Center.

Otto Luening: FANTASY IN SPACE (1952); Folkways FX 6160
        @ $4.98.
        A solo flute is the only sound source in this piece,
and the texture is varied by the addition of layers of
reverberation. Reverberation is similar to an echo and it
can be produced mechanically by using two tape recorders.
Whatever is recorded on one channel is added to another
channel a fraction of a second later. This process may be
repeated many times, so that as many layers of reverberation
as desired may be used.

Vladimir Ussachevsky: TRANSPOSITION, REVERBERATION,
        COMPOSITION, UNDERWATER WALTZ (1951-52); Folkways
        FX 6160 @ $4.98.
        These four works are based on the same sound mate-
rials. TRANSPOSITION consists of a single piano tone--the
lowest 'A' on the piano (27.5 Hz)--which is then played at
various speeds on a tape recorder. Sounds both above and
below the normal piano range are then possible. REVERBERA-
TION is simply the addition of reverberation (echo) to the
existing piece TRANSPOSITION. COMPOSITION uses the same
sounds of TRANSPOSITION, while UNDERWATER WALTZ exploits the
materials of REVERBERATION.

Vladimir Ussachevsky: OF WOOD AND BRASS (1965); CRI S-227
        @ $5.95.
        Although Ussachesvky used conventional wood and brass
instruments as the sound sources in this work, he did not
want the final tape to sound as if it had been composed of
these instrumental sounds. In order to accomplish this he
relied on the techniques of tape splicing and manipulation.
The piece is in four sections, with each section having a
different instrument as its source of sound:
        section 1 = trombone.
        section 2 = single flourish on trumpet.
        section 3 = xylophone.
        section 4 = trombone glissando and Korean
                    wood gong.

        John Cage was one of the first composers in America
to become involved with electronic music. In addition, his
study of Oriental philosophy led him to the use of chance
operations in his music, and the IMAGINARY LANDSCAPE NO. 5
(1951) is a good example of both these attitudes. In this
piece a tape is prepared by recording sections from any 42
phonograph records. The choice of records is up to the person making the tape. The only instructions given are con-
cerning the tape splicing, but they were derived from the
I-Ching Book of Changes. This book is over 2500 years old,
and it comes from China. Its purpose is to help people in
making wise decisions, and it involves the interpretation of
hexagrams in order to acquire this wisdom.

John Cage: WILLIAMS MIX (1952); Avakian JCS-1 @ $25
        (3-record set).
        Another instance of chance operations is to be found
in this piece. It consists of six categories of sound:
1) city sounds, 2) country, 3) electronic, 4) manually produced (including any music already written), 5) wind produced, and 6) small sounds requiring amplification. The
I-Ching Book of Changes was again used to establish the
splices and tape loops to be employed.

        The last composition to be discussed in this chapter
is by the American Steve Reich. The entire piece is built
upon the voice, similar to the two works of Berio covered
earlier.

Steve Reich: COME OUT (1966); Odyssey 32160160 @ $2.92.
        The title of this work comes from the phrase "come
out to show them," and this phrase is the basis of the whole
piece. It was spoken by a young Black as he was describing
how he was beat up in the Harlem 28th Precinct. As the
phrase is repeated mechanical reverberation is added in the
manner that was described earlier in connection with

-18-

Luening's FANTASY IN SPACE. Eventually the layers of reverberation become so thick that the piece is gradually transformed into a type of canon or round.

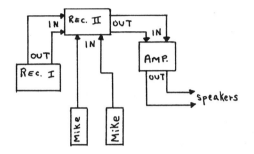

Chapter V

EXERCISES IN COMPOSITION

        This section consists of some practical exercises in
the composition of musique concrète pieces. It is important
for the student to thoroughly master the techniques of tape
manipulation at the beginning, for these have the capability
of greatly enhancing one's basic sound materials. It is
also recommended that the student do as many of the following exercises as possible, and interested students should
create their own compositional studies in addition to those
given here. Since the following studies are arranged
according to technical difficulty their succession should be
followed by the student.

        The following materials will be needed in order to do
the exercises:
        2 stereo tape recorders (3-3/4 and 7-1/2 ips)
        1 microphone
        2 5-inch reels of recording tape (Scotch 150 or 201)
        2 empty 5-inch reels
        1 splicing block and razor blade or a splicing
            machine
        splicing tape
        blank leader tape
        marking pen.

EX. 1 - Changing Tape Speeds.
        Record a person speaking a repeating succession of
words (it need not be a sentence nor follow any grammatical
conventions, e.g. help run slide pretty sad bad mad
run fun anxious capable go).

        a - Place the microphone approximately 5-6 inches from
            the speaker.
        b - Set the speed of the tape recorder to 3-3/4 ips.
        c - Set the volume control on the tape recorder so that
            the needle on the VU meter does not pass into the
            upper third of the meter when the person is speaking.

d - Instruct the speaker as to the speed, loudness, and number of repetitions that he is to make.
e - Record this material.
f - Rewind the tape and play it back at 7-1/2 ips.

EX. 2 - Playing the Tape Backwards.
    Using the tape produced in EX. 1, transfer it from the left to the right reel by playing the tape forward in the normal manner.

    a - Reverse the reels so that the right reel (now with the tape) is placed on the left side of the tape recorder, and the remaining reel is used as the pick-up reel on the right side of the machine.
    b - Play the tape forward in the normal manner--first at 3-3/4 ips, then at 7-1/2 ips.

EX. 3 - Splicing.
    Splicing is the technique of cutting and taping together pieces of recording tape, and it is best done with a splicing block and a razor blade. If these materials are not available a splicing machine may be used instead.

    Both the splicing block and machine have two possible types of cuts--diagonal and perpendicular (/ and |)--and the diagonal cut should always be used when a smooth transition is desired. The perpendicular cut may result in a click at the union of the two pieces of tape, and such sounds are to be avoided for they detract from the quality of the recording.

    a - Record (as in EX. 1) a person speaking the following words:
            rain   pretty   out   exercise   fly
        Make the recording at 7-1/2 ips.
    b - Rewind the tape and play it back. Stop after the word 'out,' and use the marking pen to mark the glossy side of the tape. (In order to do this properly one must locate the play-back head on the recorder and make all marks on the tape in reference to the play-back head. Most recorders have the following head arrangement--erase, record, playback.)
    c - Continue playing back the tape until the word 'exercise' is spoken. Stop, and make another mark on the tape as done in the previous step. Be sure only to write on the glossy side of the tape. The tape should now be as follows:

| fly | exercise | out pretty rain |

d - If the recorder has an 'EDIT' button switch to this
    position. If not, procede to the next step.
e - Manually turn both reels so that the tape becomes
    loose with some slack.
f - Place one of the marked places on the tape on the
    splicing block and make a diagonal cut. Then do the
    same with the other marked place.
g - There are now three pieces of tape, one of which is
    not connected to either reel. This piece contains
    the word 'exercise,' and it is this word that is to
    be removed from the original sequence.
h - Place the two remaining loose ends on the splicing
    block (glossy side up), and bring them as close
    together as possible without overlapping. Do not
    allow any empty spaces to exist between them.

Bad   Bad   Good

i - Tape the aligned ends together with the splicing
    tape, trimming all excess with a razor blade or
    splicing machine.
j - Manually turn the two reels to remove all slack, and
    return the tape to its normal playing position.
k - Rewind the tape and play it back from the beginning,
    listening for any 'clicks' that may have resulted
    from the splice.

    The technique of splicing must be practiced until all
splices are perfectly smooth and un-noticeable.

EX. 4 - Dubbing.
    The process of dubbing involves two tape recorders,
and is simply making a copy of another tape. This procedure
is usually necessary when composing tape pieces for it
allows one to have a greater variety of choice and freedom
in working with the basic sound materials. The usefulness
of this technique will become evident during the following
exercises.

a - Connect the output of tape recorder 1 to the input of recorder 2.

b - Place the tape produced in EX. 1 on recorder 1, and a blank tape on recorder 2. Two blank pick-up reels will therefore be needed.

c - Set the volume controls on both recorders so that neither of the VU meters indicate an overload (see EX. 1-c).

d - Set the tape speed on recorder 1 at 3-3/4 and recorder 2 at 7-1/2 ips.

e - Start recorder 2 on 'RECORD' and recorder 1 on 'PLAY.' This results in the exact duplication of the original tape.

f - Rewind recorder 1 and re-set its tape speed to 7-1/2 ips.

g - Do not rewind tape 2, but insert (splice) a piece of blank leader tape at the end of the section just dubbed. Keep the tape speed set at 7-1/2 ips.

h - Start recorder 2 on 'RECORD' and recorder 1 on 'PLAY.' This results in tape 2 being twice as fast and high as the original tape (see EX. 1-f).

i - Do not rewind tape 1, but reverse the reels as in EX. 2-a. Re-set the tape speed to 3-3/4 ips.

j - Insert another piece of leader tape after the material just dubbed on tape 2 (see EX. 4-g), and keep the tape speed set at 7-1/2 ips.

k - Start recorder 2 on 'RECORD' and recorder 1 on 'PLAY.' This results in tape 2 being the backward version of tape 1 (see EX. 2-b) played at the original speed of 3-3/4 ips.

l - Rewind recorder 1 and re-set its tape speed to 7-1/2 ips.

m - Insert a piece of leader tape after the material just dubbed on tape 2 (see EX. 4-g), and keep the tape speed set at 7-1/2 ips.

n - Start recorder 2 on 'RECORD' and recorder 1 on 'PLAY.' This results in tape 2 being another backward version of tape 1, but this time it is twice as fast and high as the previous version (see EX. 2-b and 4-k).

The examples discussed so far have been centered around the human voice as the source of sound, but any and all sounds may be used. The following partial list of sounds used in the compositions discussed in Chapter IV should help in giving students some ideas in thinking of their own sounds.

Ussachevsky: conventional instruments (piano, trombone, trumpet, xylophone), artificial reverberation.

Schaeffer: sound-effects records, bells, toy tops, pan
            covers, piano, vocal sounds.
Xenakis: bow drawn across objects (cardboard boxes, metal
          rods, gong), jewelry, change speed of records and
          tapes.
Berio: laughing, crying, singing, speaking, speech inflec-
        tions, isolated syllables.
Cage: city sounds, country sounds, wind sounds.

     Students should use their imagination to think of
interesting sounds to be used for tape pieces. It would
also be helpful if the students would record some sounds on
tape, and in this manner begin a sound library. Many composers and electronic studios have such libraries which have
become very extensive over the years.

     After the four preceding exercises have been mastered,
students should be encouraged to create their own tape compositions. In order to facilitate this procedure, a sample
tape piece is described here, including a step-by-step set
of instructions which may serve as a model for other tape
compositions.

EX. 5 - Tape Composition.

     1 - Determine the length of the piece. In this example
         it will be 40 seconds (40")(1).
     2 - Choose the type of sounds to be used. This piece
         will employ hand clapping, speaking, and a TV or
         radio commercial.
     3 - Draw a rough sketch of when these sounds are to take
         place. This will eventually evolve into the actual
         score. Mark the timings of all entrances and dura-
         tions, including silences. The use of graph paper
         will greatly facilitate the preparation of the score.

(1). The quote sign used in this context is always used to
      depict "seconds," and not inches.

-24-

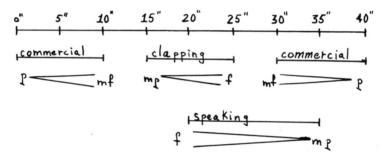

4 - Establish the dynamics of each sound, and include
    this in the score.

5 - Record all of the sounds to be used in the piece on
    the same reel of tape, separating each segment with
    a piece of blank leader tape. Make all recordings
    monaural.

    a - TV or radio commercial (20"). Since two 10"
        segments are needed it is possible to record
        only one 10" piece, and then either change the
        speed or play it backwards for the second seg-
        ment. This would provide some degree of unity,
        for both sections would resemble each other to
        some extent.
            Record a commercial of your choice using
        a microphone (see EX. 1). In order to obtain a
        change in volume from soft (p) to medium loud
        (mf) operate the volume control on the tape
        recorder, always watching the VU meter so that

it does not overload the tape recorder. Do not
change the volume of the TV or radio, but set it
between the 9 o'clock and 12 o'clock position
(☻). Place the microphone about 6 to 12
inches from the loudspeaker, and gradually
increase the volume control on the tape recorder.
Record at 7-1/2 ips.

b - Insert a piece of leader tape after this material, and proceed to make a dub by playing it
backwards (see EX. 2 and 4). Do all recording
at 7-1/2 ips. Notice that the dynamics of these
two sections are reversed, so that if the first
section is played backwards it naturally pro-
duces the dynamics of the second section.
Insert a piece of leader tape after this section.

c - Hand clapping (10"). Decide whether a single
person or a group of people are to clap their
hands. In this example a group of people will
be used. Then decide if the clapping will be
continuous or sporadic. Since this is a short
segment (10") there will be continuous clapping.
        Record as in EX. 1, and make the record-
ing at 7-1/2 ips. Operate the volume control on
the tape recorder in order to have a change in
dynamics from medium soft (mp) to loud (f).
Insert another piece of leader tape after this
section.

d - Speaking (15"). The question of how many people
take part in this segment is the same as in the
previous section. Before it is decided how many
people are needed, one should consider how this
section combines with the clapping segment. If
a group of people are used for the speaking section they combine in texture with the clapping
section.
        The choice of words that are spoken may
be left up to the group of people, so that the
effect of a crowd may be obtained. If this
crowd-effect is desired, instruct the speakers
to produce a continuous stream of sound in the
same manner as the clapping section. Control
the dynamics with the tape recorder's volume
control, and record at 7-1/2 ips.

6 - Rewind and play back (7-1/2 ips) the tape with all
of the materials and listen to each segment very
carefully, making sure that you are satisfied with
the recordings just made. Re-do any sections that
you are not perfectly satisfied with. Remember that
good recording techniques take a long time to
acquire and master, so it is well worth the extra

effort to try to achieve the highest quality
possible from the beginning.
7 - Decide which sounds are to be on either channel, and
include this in the final copy of the score (see
page 4).

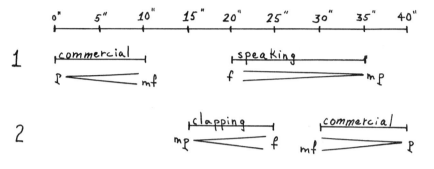

8 - Make the final copy of the tape by dubbing from the
source tape (tape I) to the new tape (tape II). The
source tape is the one that was just made, contain-
ing all of the sounds to be used in the composition.
Record each channel of the new tape separately. The
following chart shows how to carry out the dubbing
process. Refer to page 4 for stereo recording procedures, and EX. 4 for dubbing procedures.

    a - Tape I (commercial)--Tape II, channel 1 (0"-10")
    b - STOP
    c - SILENCE - allow Tape II to run for 10". (10"-20")
    d - STOP
    e - Tape I (speaking)----Tape II, channel 1 (20"-35")
    f - STOP
    g - Rewind Tape II, and set up for recording on
        channel 2 of Tape II.
    h - SILENCE - allow Tape II to run for 15". (0"-15")
    i - Tape I (clapping)---Tape II, channel 2 (15"-25")
    j - STOP
    k - SILENCE - allow Tape II to run for 5". (25"-30")
    l - Tape I (commercial--Tape II, channel 2 (30"-40")
        backwards)

    After completing the exercises up to this point the
student should be in a position where he is able to compose
a short musique concrète piece on his own. In order to make
this process as easy as possible students may base some of

-27-

their compositions on those discussed in Chapter IV. The
following list is included for this purpose.

1. Henry: VARIATIONS FOR A DOOR AND A SIGH - short sec-
           tions, all having related sound sources.
2. Henry: LE VOYAGE - individual sections based on some
           book or text.
3. Ferrari: VISAGE V - form based on fairy tale or short
             story.
4. Xenakis: BOHOR I - continuous and gradual crescendo or
             decrescendo.
5. Berio: OMAGGIO A JOYCE - based on the reading of a
           text, possibly in different languages.
6. Cage: WILLIAMS MIX - use some chance methods to make
          decisions, such as rolling dice or the I-Ching
          Book of Changes.
7. Ussachevsky: TRANSPOSITION, REVERBERATION, COMPOSITION,
                 UNDERWATER WALTZ - same sound source.

Chapter VI

DISCOGRAPHY

This chapter contains a complete listing of all records discussed in this book, in addition to some others which may be used as supplementary materials.

George Antheil: BALLET MECANIQUE, Urania 5134 @ $5.98.

Robert Ashley: WOLFMAN, ESP Disk 1009 @ $4.98.

Luciano Berio: OMAGGIO A JOYCE, Turnabout TV 34177 @ $2.98.
                VISAGE, Turnabout TV 34046 @ $2.98; Columbia
                    OS-3320 @ $5.98.
                MOMENTI, Limelight LS 86047 @ $5.98.

John Cage: VARIATIONS IV, Everest 3132 @ $4.98.
            WILLIAMS MIX, Avakian JCS-1 @ $25 (3-record set).
            CARTRIDGE MUSIC, Mainstream MS 5015 @ $4.98;
                    Time S 8009 @ $5.98.
            ARIA WITH FONTANA MIX, Mainstream MS 5005
                            @ $4.98; Time S 8003
                            @ $5.98.
            FONTANA MIX, Turnabout TV 34046 @ $2.98.

Francois Dufrene & Jean Baronnet: U 47, Limelight LS 86047
                            @ $5.98.

Luc Ferrari: VISAGE V, Limelight LS 86047 @ $5.98.
              TETE ET QUEUE DE DRAGON, Candide 31025 @ $3.98.

Pierre Henry: LA REINE VERTE, Limelight LS 86065 @ $5.98.
               ENTITE, Limelight LS 86048 @ $5.98.
               APOCALYPSE DE JEAN, Philips 837923/25
                            @ $17.94.
               MASS FOR TODAY, Limelight LS 86065 @ $5.98.
               TAM TAM IV, ASTROLOGIE, ANTIPHONIE,
               VOCALISES, DUC-9 @ $5.98.
               LE VOYAGE, Limelight LS 86049 @ $5.98.

VARIATIONS FOR A DOOR AND A SIGH, Limelight
LS 86059
@ $5.98.

Mauricio Kagel: TRANSICION I, Limelight LS 86048 @ $5.98.
TRANSICION II, Mainstream MS 5003 @ $4.98;
Time S 8001 @ $5.98.

György Ligeti: ARTIKULATION, Limelight 86048 @ $5.98.

Otto Luening: FANTASY IN SPACE, Folkways FX 6160 @ $4.98.

Bruno Maderna: CONTINUO, Limelight LS 86047 @ $5.98.

W. A. Mozart: ADAGIO IN C (K.617a), QUINTET IN C (K.617)
(both for glass harmonica), Turnabout
TV 34213/4
@ $5.96.

Henri Pousseur: SCAMBI, Limelight LS 86048 @ $5.98.

Steve Reich: COME OUT, Odyssey 32160160 @ $2.92.

Ottorino Respighi: PINES OF ROME, Columbia MS 6587 @ $5.98.

Pierre Schaeffer: ETUDE AUX ANIMES, ETUDE AUX ALLURES,
BAM LD 070 @ $4.98.
ETUDE AUX OBJETS, Philips (Eur) 835487 AY
@ $5.98.
OBJETS LIES, Candide CE 31025 @ $3.98.
ETUDE PTHETIQUE, DUC-8 @ $5.98.
LE VOILE D'ORPHEE, Suprphon DV 6221
@ $6.98.

Pierre Schaeffer & Pierre Henry: SYMPHONIE POUR UN HOMME
SEUL, DUC-9 @ $5.98.

Karlheinz Stockhausen: MIKROPHONIE I, Columbia MS 7355
@ $5.98.

Vladimir Ussachevsky: OF WOOD AND BRASS, CRI S-227 @ $5.95.
WIRELESS FANTASY, CRI S-228 @ $5.95.
SONIC CONTOURS, Desto DC 6466 @ $5.98
Folkways FX 6160
@ $4.98.
PIECE FOR TAPE RECORDER, CRI 112
@ $5.95.
TRANSPOSITION, REVERBERATION, COMPOSI-
TION, UNDERWATER WALTZ, Folkways
FX 6160
@ $4.98.

Edgar Varèse: DESERTS, Columbia MS 6362 @ $5.98.
                POEME ELECTRONIQUE, Columbia MS 6146 @ $5.98.

Iannis Xenakis: ORIENT-OCCIDENT I, Limelight LS 86407
                                @ $5.98.
                  ORIENT-OCCIDENT III, BOHOR I, CONCRETE P-H
                  II, DIAMORPHOSES II, Nonesuch H 71246
                                @ $2.98.
                  PITHOPRAKTA, Nonesuch 71201 @ $2.98.

BIBLIOGRAPHY

1. Audio Devices, Inc. THE AUDIOTAPE CATALOG, New York.

2. Backus, John. THE ACOUSTICAL FOUNDATIONS OF MUSIC,
    Norton, New York, 1969.

3. Basart, Ann Philips. SERIAL MUSIC: A CLASSIFIED
    BIBLIOGRAPHY ON WRITINGS ON TWELVE-TONE AND ELECTRONIC
    MUSIC, University of California Press, Cal., 1961.

4. Cage, John. SILENCE, M.I.T. Press, Conn., 1961.

5. Crowhurst, Norman. ABC'S OF TAPE RECORDING,
    Indianapolis, Ind.

6. Hansen, Peter S. AN INTRODUCTION TO TWENTIETH CENTURY
    MUSIC, Allyn and Bacon, Boston, Mass., 1971.

7. Jorgensen, Finn. HANDBOOK OF MAGNETIC TAPE RECORDING,
    New York.

8. Judd, F. C. ELECTRONIC MUSIC AND MUSIQUE CONCRETE,
    London, 1961.

9. Krenek, Ernst. NEW DEVELOPMENT IN ELECTRONIC MUSIC,
    Musical America, 75:8 (Sept. 1955).

10. Lincoln, Harry B. THE COMPUTER AND MUSIC, Cornell
    University Press, Ithaca, N. Y., 1970.

11. MUSIC EDUCATORS JOURNAL, (Nov. 1968).

12. Revere-Mincom Division. CREATIVE TEACHING WITH TAPE,
    Minn.

13. Revere-Mincom Division. HOW TO DO IT BOOKLET OF TAPE
    RECORDING, Minn.

14. Revere-Mincom Division. 101 TERMS - A GLOSSARY OF TAPE
    RECORDING TERMS, Minn.

15. Revere-Mincom Division.   RECORDING BASICS, Minn.

16. Rossi, Nick and Choate, Robert.   MUSIC OF OUR TIME,
    Crescendo, Boston.

17. Tall, Joel.   MUSIC WITHOUT MUSICIANS, Saturday Review,
    40:56-57 (Jan. 26, 1957).

18. Winckel, Fritz.   MUSIC, SOUND AND SENSATION, Dover, New
    York, 1967.

19. Wood, Alexander.   THE PHYSICS OF MUSIC, Methuen & Co.,
    London, 1965.

INDEX

Allgemeine Elektrizitäts Gesellschaft, 7, 9
amplitude, 1
Antheil, George, 7, 9, 29
  BALLET MECANIQUE, 7,9,29
Art of Noises, 7, 9
Ashley, Robert, 29
  WOLFMAN, 29

Baronnet, Jean, 29
  U 47, 29
Beethoven, 6
Béjart, Maurice, 11, 12
Bell, Alexander, 6, 9
Berio, Luciano, 8, 14, 15, 24, 28, 29
  MOMENTI, 29
  OMAGGIO A JOYCE, 15, 29
  VISAGE, 15, 29
Brussels World Fair, 13, 17

Cage, John, 7, 9, 18, 24, 28, 29
  ARIA WITH FONTANA MIX, 29
  CARTRIDGE MUSIC, 29
  FONTANA MIX, 29
  IMAGINARY LANDSCAPE NO. 1, 7, 9
  IMAGINARY LANDSCAPE NO. 5, 18
  VARIATIONS IV, 29
  WILLIAMS MIX, 18, 29
carillon, 6, 9
de Caus, 6, 9
Columbia-Princeton Center, 16
Composition exercises, 20-27
computer, 3
CPS, 1

Degottex, 12
Dufrene, Francois, 29
  U 47, 29

echo, 17
Edison, Thomas, 6, 7, 9

Ferrari, Luc, 13, 14, 29
  TETE ET QUEUE DE DRAGON, 29
  VISAGE V, 13, 29
filter, 15
Franklin, Benjamin, 6, 9
Frequency, 1, 2

Glass harmonica, 6, 9, 30

Henry, Pierre, 11-14, 28, 29
  ANTIPHONIE, 11, 29
  APOCALYPSE DE JEAN, 29
  ASTROLOGIE, 11, 29
  ENTITE, 12, 29
  LA REINE VERTE, 29
  LE VOYAGE, 11-13, 28, 29
  MASS FOR TODAY, 11, 29
  TAM TAM IV, 29
  VARIATIONS FOR A DOOR AND A SIGH, 11, 12, 30
  VOCALISES, 29
hydraulic organ, 6, 9
Hz, 1

I-Ching Book of Changes, 1 , 28
input, 3
Intonarumori, 7

Joyce, James, 15
  ULYSSES, 15

Kagel, Mauricio, 30
  TRANSICION I, 30
  TRANSICION II, 30
Köln, 13, 15, 17

Le Corbusier, 13
Ligeti, György, 30
  ARTIKULATION, 30
Luening, Otto, 17, 30
  FANTASY IN SPACE, 17, 30

Maderna, Bruno, 30
  CONTINUO, 30
microphone, 3, 4, 15, 16, 20
Milan, 13, 15
Milhaud, Darius, 7, 9
Mozart, 6, 30
  ADAGIO IN C, 30
  QUINTET IN C, 30

-35-

output, 4

Paris, 6, 10
phonograph, 6, 9
Philips Pavilion, 13, 17
pianola, 7, 9
Pousseur, Henri, 30
  SCAMBI, 30

Radiodiffusion-Television Francaise, 10, 13, 16
Reich, Steve, 18, 30
  COME OUT, 18, 30
Respighi, Ottorino, 7, 9, 30
  PINES OF ROME, 7, 9, 30
Russolo, Luigi, 7, 9

Schaeffer, Pierre, 6, 9-11, 24, 30
  ETUDE AU PIANO I, 10
  ETUDE AU PIANO II, 10
  ETUDE AUX ANIMES, 30
  ETUDE AUX CASSEROLES, 10
  ETUDE AUX CHEMINS DE FER, 10
  ETUDE AUX OBJETS, 30
  ETUDE AUX TOURNIQUETS, 10
  ETUDE PATHETIQUE, 30
  LE VOILE D'ORPHEE, 30
  OBJETS LIES, 30
stereo, 4, 5
Stockhausen, Karlheinz, 8, 15, 16, 30
  MIKROPHONIE I, 15, 30
  SYMPHONIE POUR UN HOMME SEUL, 11
synthesiser, 3

tape recorder, 3-5, 9
telephone, 6, 9
Tibetan Book of the Dead, 12

UNESCO, 14
Ussachevsky, Vladimir, 17, 18, 23, 28, 30
  COMPOSITION, 17, 28, 30
  OF WOOD AND BRASS, 18, 30
  PIECE FOR TAPE RECORDER, 30
  REVERBERATION, 17, 28, 30
  SONIC CONTOURS, 17, 28, 30
  TRANSPOSITION, 17, 28, 30
  UNDERWATER WALTZ, 17, 28, 30
  WIRELESS FANTASY, 30

Varèse, Edgar, 14, 16, 17, 31
  DESERTS, 16, 31
  POEM ELECTRONIQUE, 17, 31
Vortez, 7, 9
VU meter, 5

waves, 1

Xenakis, Iannis, 13, 14, 17, 24, 28, 32
  BOHOR I, 14, 28, 32
  CONCRETE P-H II, 13, 17, 32
  DIAMORPHOSES II, 14, 32
  ORIENT-OCCIDENT I, 14, 32
  ORIENT-OCCIDENT III, 14, 32
  PITHOPRAKTA, 14, 32

David Ernst is both a composer and pianist, specializing in the areas of electronic music and improvisation. Following a graduate teaching assistantship at Rutgers, he was assistant professor of music at San Diego State College where he taught their first courses in electronic music, and is now at York College, Jamaica, N. Y.

One of his first compositions involving electronics was *FOUR AND MORE,* written for percussion quartet and two tape recorders. It received its premiere at the International Music Week in the Netherlands (1968) sponsored by the Foundation Gaudeamus, and published in New York by MUSIC FOR PERCUSSION.

In addition to composing and teaching, Mr. Ernst gives lectures on various aspects of electronic music, and has organized an improvisation ensemble in which electronic sounds and tapes are an integral part of the overall structure of the music.